Reids' Hotel

JEWEL OF THE ATLANTIC

The original, main building of Reid's Hotel, designed by George Somers Clarke and J. Micklethwaite.

Reid's Hotel

JEWEL OF THE ATLANTIC

1891–1991

H. J. WEAVER

SOUVENIR PRESS

First published 1991 by Souvenir Press Ltd,
43 Great Russell Street, London WC1B 3PA
and simultaneously in Canada

ISBN 0 285 63032 6

Printed in Great Britain by
Redwood Press Limited, Melksham, Wiltshire

Acknowledgements

I should like to thank Richard and Michael Blandy, both directors and present owners of Reid's Hotel, for their generous hospitality; the courteous and always helpful hotel staff, and, in particular, Urs Bührer and his assistant, Marie-Hélène Jung, for their willing co-operation in supplying documents and information concerning the hotel's history, both past and present; Brenda Brainch, for making available her valuable research into the story of Reid's; Michael Holroyd, whose third volume of Bernard Shaw's biography, *Bernard Shaw: The Lure of Fantasy*, is to be published in this centenary year; Photographia-Museu Vicentes of Funchal for the supply of black-and-white photographs; Ana Isabel S. F. Dantas of the Madeira Wine Co; and David Higham Associates for permission to quote from *Portugal and Madeira* by the late Sir Sacheverell Sitwell, published by Batsford.

H.J.W.

Contents

Photo: Alexes Weaver

There are many hotels, there are few good hotels, there is only one Reid's Hotel.

Prince Leon of Lignac,
Duke of Soveria Simeri.

(*Entry in the visitors' Golden Book at Reid's Hotel*)

A Dream of Perfection

1

A Dream of Perfection

MADEIRA was discovered in 1418 by the Portuguese explorer Gonsalves Zarco, during an expedition under the patronage of Prince Henry the Navigator. The prince, third son of a fifteenth-century King of Portugal, was not himself a navigator—the farthest he ever strayed from his native land was to Tangier in North Africa—but he was the inspiration behind a whole series of expeditions in search of new territories that could be acquired in the name of Portugal.

On an earlier expedition, Zarco had been blown off course by a violent storm. He had found sanctuary on a tiny Atlantic island, which he named Porto Sancto—today known as Porto Santo—in thanksgiving for having reached a safe, blessed port after days of bad weather. Now his aim was to try to find the cause of the clouds which gathered from time to time on the horizon to the south-west of Porto Santo. It was not a popular decision with most of his crew, who took the view that the mysterious clouds marked the end of a flat world

and that they would simply sail off the edge of it and plunge into a bottomless pit. Their fears proved unduly pessimistic. Beneath the clouds they found a green and pleasant island so covered with trees that Zarco named it Madeira, the Portuguese for 'wood'. Once ashore, he founded the first settlement at a spot on the coast which he called Funchal, inspired by the *funcho* (fennel) growing there in abundance.

The new island of Madeira was colonised, and with the passing of the centuries it played host to many famous men, including Christopher Columbus, shortly after his marriage in 1478 to Felipa Perestrello e Montez, the daughter of the governor of Porto Santo and a member of one of Portugal's leading families . . . Captain James Cook, the British explorer, on the first voyage of his ship, the *Endeavour*, which led to the discovery of New Zealand in 1769 and Australia in 1770 . . . Napoleon in 1815 when HMS *Northumberland*, the British naval vessel taking him to the remote island of

REID'S HOTELS (Established 1850),

BY APPOINTMENT TO H.R.H. THE DUKE OF EDINBURGH.

SANTA CLARA HOTEL.—"Admirably situated, overlooking Funchal; fine view of the mountains and sea."—*Vide Rendell's Guide to Madeira.*

REID'S NEW HOTEL.—Situated on the Cliffs to the west of Funchal, on the New Road, overlooking the Sea, grand view of the Mountains. Sea Bathing and Boating.

MILES'S CARMO HOTEL.—In sheltered central position.

HORTAS HOTEL.—German spoken. Splendid position.

SANT' ANNA HOTEL.—Good centre for scenery of the interior and north of Island.

These **first-class** Hotels afford every comfort for families and travellers. Excellent Cuisine and Choice Wines. Tennis Courts, large Gardens, Baths, Reading and Smoking Rooms, English and German Newspapers. Billiards. The Sanitary arrangements have been carried out by the Banner Sanitation Company, of London. All Steamers met.

There is an absolute freedom from dust in Madeira.

Telegraphic Address:
" Reid, Funchal."

Pamphlet free—apply to
WILLIAM REID.

Advertisement for Reid's New Hotel in *A Guide to the Canary Islands and Madeira* by Ellebeck (1892).

St Helena for his second spell in exile, anchored off Funchal to take on board supplies of fruit, books and Madeira wine.

Not surprisingly, nobody in Madeira had heard of William Reid when he first stepped ashore at Funchal in 1836. He was fourteen years of age, one of twelve children of a Scottish farmer, and not in good health. The family doctor had therefore recommended that he should be sent to live and seek his fortune in a warmer climate. With just £5 in his pocket, he worked his way—probably as a cabin boy—to Funchal via Lisbon and, true to the traditions of Scottish thrift, still had his £5 intact when he set foot on Madeiran soil. Five pounds was, of course, worth a good deal more then than it is now, but it was still a modest sum with which to start a new life in a foreign land. Yet, by the turn of the century, the name of Reid was already becoming a household word to people of discernment, not for discoveries he had made or battles he had fought, but for the hotel he had created, a hotel whose style and elegance made it a rival to Raffles in Singapore, Shepheard's in Cairo and the Ritz in London, as a playground of royalty, the rich and the famous.

*   *   *

The new hotel that William Reid built—but, sadly, did not live to see open its doors in November 1891, three years after his death at the age of sixty-six—was set on a promontory, one hundred and fifty feet above the Atlantic, with splendid views over the sea, Funchal harbour and the steep green hills of Madeira, dotted with white houses topped by bright red roofs. At the time, William Reid's two sons, Willy and Alfred, styling themselves 'Hotel Keepers and Wine Merchants by Appointment to the Duke of Saxe-Coburg and Gotha (HRH Duke of Edinburgh)' wrote a guide called *Madeira* in which they explained:

'The bathing here is perfect,' declared the Reid brothers in their guide to the new hotel's amenities. The rock pool at the base of the cliff remained the hotel's only swimming pool until the opening of the new wing in 1967. *Photo: Museu Vicentes*

The hotel is constructed in sets of single and suites of rooms, with separate balconies, at different levels, with large public entertainment and sitting-rooms.

The terraces in front wind along the margin of the sea, one hundred feet above the blue water. There is splendid drinking water, and grounds, which cover several acres, contain tennis courts and various interests. The large verandah outside the drawing-room is a beautiful lounge, and the smoking room is near at hand. A winding-way leads to the rocks beneath, which above are gay with the native flora, and washed with the pure Atlantic below. The bathing here is perfect, and we contemplate enlarging the present pools, into which the tides now flow, to make this bathing—

the great want of Funchal—an especially prominent feature in our new business.

They went on to outline the precise routine of hotel life at their new establishment, starting with early morning tea and light refreshments and followed by:

9 a.m.	Breakfast (*table d'hôte*)
11 a.m.	Broth, beef tea, etc. for invalids
1 p.m.	Luncheon (*table d'hôte*)
4.30 p.m.	Tea in the drawing-room
7 p.m.	Dinner

They were, they said,

particularly fortunate in our local supplies of food. Our beef and veal are excellent, and there is a constant tendency to improvement in our breeds of sheep. Our hams and bacon are imported from an English country farm. Our supplies of fresh eggs, milk and butter are constant, and there is no season of the year in which our tables do not abound with a great variety of fresh vegetables and fruits, of many of which we are the sole growers ... It is no easy thing in a northern country to conceive the appearance of our dining-tables in the winter season, decked profusely with flowers, and served unstintedly with the delicate greenhouse produce of an English summer. Our winter fruits include the orange, the custard apple, mango and alligator pear, strawberries, the guava of several kinds, the loquats, apples, pears and walnuts, besides imported dried fruits. Gooseberries and cherries appear in spring as in England, but earlier, but in summer our markets furnish many varieties of plums, apricots, figs and peaches. Bananas are in season all the year round.

The cost of living in such comfort and feasting so magnificently varied, of course, with the size of rooms and the extent of the accommodation, but, said the Reids' guide, terms 'may be generally stated as from £12 upwards for a single bedroom for the period of four weeks, inclusive of *table d'hôte* meals and light refreshments, and the use of public rooms and general advantages.' Double rooms with meals for the same period cost from £22. 4s. 6d. (£22.22½ in today's decimal currency), a servant's room with meals £6. However, these prices have to be seen in the light of the fact that a skilled engineering worker in Britain at this period was expected to work nearly sixty hours a week for a modest £1. 10s. 0d. (£1.50) and a farmworker's pay for similar hours was a mere 12s. 0d. (60p), a situation which was hardly better in other European countries. With telegrams from Britain to Funchal costing 1s. 3d. (just over 6p) a word, the Reid brothers remembered their thrifty Scottish ancestry by including at the front of their guide a code which enabled potential guests to save money by simply naming the ship on which they proposed to travel and securing their room reservations by codewords such as Single (single bedroom), Homely (two double bedrooms), Follower (sitting and double bedroom and servant's room) and, although they can hardly have been short of the price of a telegram, Clergy for those guests who required a sitting-room, two double bedrooms, two single bedrooms and two servant's rooms.

*   *   *

In the early days, when roads were scarce and cobbled, visitors to Madeira going shopping or making excursions to the island's interior usually hired a hammock, carried by two or three men according to the weight of the passenger. The Reid brothers reassured guests in their guidebook that the hammocks were 'most ably handled by muscular and gentle bearers, to the great advantage of delicate people, who are thus enabled to spend their entire days in passive, unfatiguing exercise. These conveyances can be . . . hired for the hour or longer periods at nearly the same rates as sledges or horses; monthly, £5. 10s. (£5.50) to £6.' Another guidebook of the period recommended visitors to favour the hammocks of the Tourist Excursion Company, which used them 'for trips to the Grand Curral and other beauty spots in the interior . . . the Tourist Company employ their own bearers and are thus able to reduce prices to a minimum. When touring the island, visitors should always make inquiries at the country agencies of this Company, when lowest quotations and trustworthy bearers will be forthcoming.'

Daisy Esplay, Reid's housekeeper, in a hammock, in about 1908.

One of the very few complaints to be found in the book that Reid's keeps for this purpose was voiced on 3 January, 1938, by a Mrs Elaine Winans. She protested: 'I find it impossible to obtain any sleep after seven o'clock in the morning owing to the unnecessary noise and shouting made by the drivers of the bullock and mule carts. Is it possible to do something about this?'

Even at this comparatively late date, the *carro*—a kind of sledge with greased wooden runners—was still the most common form of transport to be seen in the cobbled streets of Madeira and was used both for the delivery of goods and as a taxi that could carry up to four passengers. It was drawn as a rule by bullocks although mules took their place if a speedier journey was called for. The conveyance was guided by a *carro* man while a small boy ran ahead, urging the creatures drawing it to greater efforts as if they could understand speech. Despite the fact that it was running over cobbles, the *carro* provided a surprisingly smooth ride.

Times have changed. Today Reid's imports a great deal of European foodstuffs by air as well as sea—from Britain around 1.5 tons a year of fresh Scottish salmon, which is smoked in the hotel's own oven, 0.5 tons of venison, pheasant, grouse and partridge; from France beef, veal and lamb (6 tons), fish and seafood (2.8 tons), vegetables and fruit (2 tons) and fresh goose-liver (0.2 tons); and from Germany marzipan, flour and chocolate.

Of local produce, guests consume around 5 tons a year of the popular *espada* fish, a similar amount of bananas, 1.5 tons of Madeira cake—and, as an aperitif or accompaniment to their meals, some 3,000 bottles of Madeira wine.

A bullock-drawn sledge delivers supplies to the Villa Victoria, an annexe of Reid's Hotel.
Photo: Museu Vicentes

Today the quality of service and comfort remains of the highest. The Irish bedlinen in the hotel rooms is changed every day, towels as soon as it is discovered that they have been used. This ensures that the hotel laundry is never short of work. Each day, among other items, it deals with 400 sheets, 1,000 towels and 300 tablecloths.

The building of Reid's New Hotel was intended by William Reid as the climax to a career which had turned out to be far more successful than he can ever have dreamed when he first set foot on Madeira with £5 in his pocket. He found a job almost at once in a German bakery, where he was poorly paid and had to work long hours at night, but he saved what he could and, when he felt he had enough money behind him, turned his back on baking and sought a niche in the flourishing Madeira wine trade. This proved such a successful venture that by 1847, at the age of twenty-five, he owned a small wine-exporting company and was seeking means of expanding his business interests.

It was not necessary to look far. Madeira is reputed to have one of the finest climates in the world, with summer temperatures rarely soaring above 27°C (87°F) and winter temperatures never sinking below 10°C (52°F). Between October and February, rain falls on average on only about six days a month. Doctors were enthusiastic advocates of the island as an ideal choice for anyone who wished to escape from northern winter fogs and freezing temperatures, and recommended Madeira to patients suffering from a wide variety of complaints, including tuberculosis, laryngitis, bronchitis, several forms of renal disease, catarrh, persistent fevers and chronic Bright's disease, whose sufferers 'derived obvious benefit where a harsh dry skin had been a prominent symptom'. The authoritative British medical journal *The Lancet* also recommended the island as 'a stepping stone by consumptive patients on their way to a more vigorous atmosphere. In all probability there is no warm country in the world where the irritating influence of wind and dust is so completely absent as in Madeira.' Even men who had nothing worse wrong with them than feeling tired from too much work were recommended to take a break on the island.

In the circumstances it was not surprising that many families, accompanied by servants, grooms and some-

Girls in traditional costume in the garden of Reid's Hotel, from the cover of an Easter dinner menu, 1958.

times even their own furniture, chose to spend the whole winter season, from October to the end of June, in Madeira, where a *quinta*—a spacious dwelling house in its own grounds—could be rented for as little as £40. Letting and managing *quintas* proved the next business venture for William Reid, an enterprise which led to love, marriage and, eventually, a career as a hotelier. One of his earliest customers was a Marchioness Camden, who rented a *quinta* for two years. With her she brought a travelling companion named Margaret Dewey. William Reid promptly fell in love with this young woman and they were married in 1847, when he was twenty-five and she twenty-eight.

At the time, Madeira had few actual hotels, and in view of the ever-increasing popularity of the island, William Reid and his bride decided there was money to be made by putting this right. They bought the Quinta

William Reid (back row, second from right) with members of his extensive family. In all he fathered twelve children, several of whom died in infancy or childhood.

das Fontes, a fine house set between the public gardens of Funchal and the sea. Twenty years later the Hotel das Fontes was renamed the Royal Edinburgh Hotel by permission of Alfred, Duke of Edinburgh, second son of Queen Victoria of England, who had made frequent calls at Madeira during his years as an officer in the Royal Navy and had struck up a firm friendship with William Reid, whom he called 'Auld Reekie'. By this time, William Reid was the owner of two other hotels, the Carmo and the Santa Clara. The latter commanded a fine view across Funchal Bay and was on the opposite side of a cobbled street from Santa Clara Convent, where Gonsalves Zarco, the discoverer of Madeira, is buried. He had also acquired a number of boarding-houses. Yet for another twenty years he nursed a dream of building still another hotel, designed to his own specifications, which would be the finest on the island—indeed, would be renowned as one of the finest in the world. He knew exactly where he wanted to build it. Unfortunately, the site already belonged to somebody else.

Floral Paradise

Previous page: Panoramic view of Reid's Hotel, with its new extensions and improvements. From a 1990 painting by Polly Raynes.

Right: The hotel's main entrance. *Photo: Andreas von Einsiedel*

Below: View over Funchal Bay from Reid's Hotel gardens.

Left: The swimming pools, seen from the hotel.

Below: Swimming in the rock pool.

Photos: Andreas von Einsiedel

Right: The main restaurant, with its redecorated ceiling.

Below: The tea terrace.

Below right: The gourmet restaurant, Les Faunes.

Photos: Andreas von Einsiedel

2

Floral Paradise

To THE west of Funchal, above a deep ravine, stands a rocky promontory called the Salto de Cavalo. The more he looked at it, the more convinced William Reid became that this was the ideal site for the hotel of his dreams. Yet it was already graced by a *quinta* and its outbuildings belonging to a legendary Madeiran figure, Dr Michael Comport Grabham.

Dr Grabham, who had been born in Essex in 1840, was a man of many parts—a senior fellow of the Royal College of Physicians in London, the owner of two hundred clocks (the clock of Funchal Cathedral was presented by him), and a sufficiently talented organist to have been invited to play in St Paul's Cathedral, London. William Reid was able to persuade him to sell the site on the promontory, otherwise Reid's Hotel would almost certainly not have been built with the commanding views it enjoys today. Dr Grabham proved an excellent advertisement for Madeira's beneficial climate and lived on for the better part of half a

century until his death in 1935 at the age of ninety-five.

Once he had acquired Dr Grabham's *quinta*, William Reid lost no time in realising his dream. Firstly, there was the question of an architect. The new owner of the site had no hesitation in appointing George Somers Clarke, a distinguished architect, antiquarian and ecclesiologist whose design for the recently-completed Shepheard's Hotel in Cairo—he lived there largely for health reasons—had been widely acclaimed, and his partner, J. Micklethwaite. They started work on their designs in 1887. It was also part of William Reid's plan that his guests would not only have the benefit of first-class accommodation and quality cuisine, allied to impeccable service, but would be able to stroll and sun themselves in a beautiful garden. To that end, thousands of basket-loads of rich soil were carried on the shoulders of Madeiran workers and strewn on the barren slopes of the rocky promontory. The ultimate success of this aspect of the hotel was described in

View across Funchal Bay from the rocky promontory called the Salto de Cavalo which William Reid purchased in 1887. Photographed from Reid's garden in 1951.

Reid's Hotel opened in November 1891, but did not receive its licence until 22 January, 1892. This photographed page from the records shows subsequent licence renewals up to 1896.

The ten-acre tropical garden at Reid's is a riot of colour throughout the year. It features trees from all over the world, including Brazil, China, North and South America, Australia, Africa, Korea, Japan and Mexico; flowering shrubs, including hibiscus, bougainvillea, mimosa, wistaria and rhododendron, and a rich variety of the brilliant flowers that have earned Madeira its title as the 'Garden of the Atlantic'.

glowing terms by the author of the guide *Madeira: Old and New*, published in 1909 when the garden had had time to establish itself:

> . . . it is not every hotel that is placed such as this. It stands about a mile to the west of the main town upon a lofty bluff of rock that is smothered for the most part in vegetation . . . One may reach the spot by the main road to the west, or by a launch that skirts the landing stage at the base of the rock. Close by this landing stage is the bathing pool where one can splash about in protected waters if the plunge into the deep outer ocean be beyond the taste of the unskilled swimmer.
>
> Climbing upwards, one mounts flight after flight of stone steps, each of which leads to a terrace more fascinating than the last, until one arrives at the main gardens themselves. It is a little difficult to describe these without a dangerous prodigality of adjective. Broad masses of bougainvillea of every colour from purple and scarlet to terra-cotta make splashes that stand out even from the surrounding wealth of flowers. Bigoni in golden red lanes, wistaria with its lilac blossom hovering admidst the trees, solandra with its white and gold trumpet-shaped flower, the blue and orange strelitzia regina, and the white and blue strelitzia augusta, the scarlet passion flower—these alone suffice to bewilder the eye at the first glimpse.
>
> But the number of curious growths here is legion. One may walk along a couple of miles of paths to discover hedges of rosemary, pepper trees, the great sedum with its fleshy leaves and cactus-like flower, the towering blossom of the aloe, the quaint schottia tree that sprouts its flowers direct from the branch, and hedges and stacks of geranium. Here, too, in May blooms the wonderful peacock-blue of the jacaranda—colloquially known as the peacock tree since it holds its

gorgeous blossoms aloft as proudly as does the bird its fan-like tail.

The tennis court itself is in danger of being overrun by blossoms that one sees discouraged almost with regret. More terraces, further glowing paths, and then the main building rears itself before one, with the great verandah that runs nearly its entire length, before which stretches the panorama of Funchal and of the Bay beneath in all its wealth of light and shadow.

The new hotel proved a success from the time Willy and Alfred Reid declared it open in November 1891. One of the earliest of its distinguished guests was Empress Elizabeth I of Austria, still grieving over one of the many domestic tragedies that plagued the Habsburg family. Two years before, her son, Crown Prince Rudolf, had made an assignation with one of his many mistresses, the part Greek, part Czech-Austrian Baroness Marie Vetsera, at a royal hunting lodge. There they drank champagne and brandy and made love before Rudolf shot her dead, placed a rose on her nude body, wrote a suicide note and blew his own brains out. After servants found the dead couple, Rudolf's body was taken to Vienna and his mistress's hidden in the hunting lodge at Mayerling in an effort, unsuccessful as it was to prove, to hush up the scandal. However, twenty-four hours later, two uncles of the baroness demanded her body, which they dressed, carried from the hunting lodge as if she were merely ill and drove her in a carriage to the Austrian capital where she was buried in a Cistercian abbey.

The Empress, who has been described as 'adoring travel to comparatively strange places like Madeira', chose Reid's as the place where she might learn to forget her lingering grief. The verandah of her suite overlooked the bay where ships of the Royal Navy anchored on their periodic visits to Madeira. During her stay, British naval vessels calling at the island did

Elizabeth, Empress of Austria, from a painting by Winterhalter (private collection). *Photo: The Bridgeman Art Library*

The tennis court has remained a popular amenity of the hotel. Here Diana, eldest of Winston Churchill's three daughters, partners her husband during their honeymoon at Reid's in 1932. The marriage to John Milner Bailey, eldest son of the South African industrialist Sir Abe Bailey, did not last, and in 1935 she became the wife of the British politician Duncan Sandys.

Ships of the British Navy at anchor in Funchal Bay in an earlier era, and the menu for a gala dinner dance given to commemorate the visit of HMS *Bermuda* in October 1960.

GALA DINNER DANCE

TO COMMEMORATE

THE VISIT OF

H.M.S. "BERMUDA"

REID'S HOTEL
MADEIRA

22nd October, 1960

her the honour of firing a royal salute each morning and a band played while the Austrian flag was hoisted, a courtesy the Empress—hailed as the most beautiful princess in Europe at the time of her marriage to Emperor Franz Josef—acknowledged by standing on her verandah with her dark, waist-length hair streaming down her back. Tragically, her own years were numbered: in 1898 she was stabbed and killed by an Italian anarchist.

Unfortunately, many of the records relating to the hotel's early years have been lost or destroyed and it is possible from its *Golden Book* to gain only a glimpse of its growing international popularity. Earl Roberts, the field marshal who was Commander-in-Chief of the British Army, chose to spend Christmas there in 1900 and enjoyed the experience so much that he returned for a second visit four years later. Sir Austen Chamberlain, the British statesman, took a holiday at Reid's in 1903, his first year in office as Chancellor of the Exchequer. The Duke of Connaught and Strathearn, the seventh child and third son of Britain's Queen Victoria, followed two years later. Although he did not actually stay at Reid's, Captain Robert Falcon Scott, RN, also made a visit when his ship *Discovery* called at Funchal in 1901, *en route* to his first two voyages of exploration in the Antarctic. Guests at this time tended to be largely British, although members of the Continental nobility included the German Princess Herminia de Hanan and the Italian Duchess d'Aosta.

By the time the world lurched towards the First World War, Reid's had become the centre of Madeira's gay social life. It was the custom to close the hotel down for two months in the summer, although several annexes to the main building, including the Villa Victoria, remained open in and out of season. When war finally came in August 1914, the hotel was shut—and remained shut until peace again descended upon the world four years later.

The enforced closure did nothing to diminish the popularity of Reid's. One of the first of the hotel's distinguished visitors after the eventual Armistice, following in the footsteps of his father, was Prince Arthur of Connaught, accompanied by his wife, Alexandra, a grand-daughter of Britain's King Edward VII and, in her own right, the Duchess of Fife. Shortly before his first visit to Reid's, the prince had returned from a trip to Japan surrounded by sufficient mystery to give rise to speculation, still current today, that it was connected with the rescue of the Grand Duchess Tatiana, one of the four daughters of Tsar Nicholas II, before the massacre of the family at Ekaterinburg by the Russian revolutionaries in July 1918 (see p. 65).

The following year saw the arrival into exile of ex-Emperor Karl of Austria and ex-Empress Zita, resulting from territorial adjustments which followed the end of the Great War, and the British explorer Sir Ernest Shackleton, who had first made the acquaintance of Reid's as a member of Scott's 1901–04 expedition. This, his fourth expedition to the frozen wastes of the Antartic, was to be his last: he died aboard his vessel, the *Quest*, before returning to Britain.

The hotel's *Golden Book* makes it clear that the majority of its distinguished guests in the inter-war years were still predominantly British. The Earl of Birkenhead, lawyer and statesman better known as F.E. Smith, became a regular visitor with his family during the 1920s. Today he is probably best remembered for his earlier alliance with Sir Edward Carson, the Irish politician, to organise armed resistance in Ulster against the possibility of Home Rule for Ireland. His efforts in Ulster earned him the nickname 'Galloper Smith' and, seventy years later, have left the streets of the province still stained with the blood of sectarian strife.

The Irish author George Bernard Shaw, whose many plays include *Pygmalion*, the inspiration for the internationally successful musical *My Fair Lady*, arrived in 1924, at the age of 68, to work, enjoy the sun and

The sledge drawn by bullocks was the usual form of transport in Madeira up to the Second World War. The Reid family outside the hotel in about 1908.

Prince Arthur and Princess Alexandra of Connaught during their visit to Madeira in November 1920. *Photo: Museu Vicentes*

The Earl and Countess of Birkenhead with their family at Reid's Hotel in 1930.

bathing, and to master the elusive intricacies of dancing the tango. As the years passed he was followed by David Lloyd George, who had served as Britain's War Minister and Prime Minister during the First World War, and his family . . . the third Duke of Westminster, who owned some three hundred acres of fashionable Mayfair and Belgravia in central London and was thought to be the richest man in Britain after King George V . . . the Duke of Kent . . . the Prince of Wales

On days when a tea-dance was organised for the guests, a dance floor was laid on the level surface of the tennis court.
Photo: Museu Vicentes

RECEIVED WITH THANKS, ONE EMPEROR, ONE EMPRESS

The British cruiser HMS *Cardiff* sailed from Constantinople on Friday, 4 November, 1921, at 1330 hrs and arrived at Sulina, the port at the mouth of the River Danube, at 1300 hrs on 5 November. Some twenty-eight hours later, the keeper of the log of HMS *Cardiff* noted, in the laconic way of naval logkeepers:

'1710 Romanian ship Principiza Maria secured alongside.'

The scene was set for the death throes of an empire that had lasted, in one form or another, for the better part of seven hundred years. Nearly three hours later, the same logkeeper recorded, somewhat inaccurately:

'1955 Ex-Emperor Karl of Hungary, the ex-Empress, Count and Countess Hunyadi and one attendant received on board from Principiza Maria.'

Karl I was actually Emperor of Austria and King of Hungary, last of the Habsburg rulers. In 1916, at the height of the First World War, he had inherited both thrones on the death of his great-uncle, the Emperor Franz Josef, at the venerable age of eighty-six. Karl, who was not yet thirty years of age at the time and had no experience beyond a brief army career, tried to enter into secret peace negotiations with the Allies. They failed, and once his efforts became public, compromised him in the eyes of Kaiser Wilhelm of Germany. Subsequently, in a wave of nationalist fervour, the Habsburg empire disintegrated into a group of independent states—Hungary, Czechoslovakia, the kingdom of the Croats, Serbs and Slovenes (now Yugoslavia)—who erected customs barriers against each other as well as Austria.

Karl I informed Kaiser Wilhelm at the end of October 1918 that Austria could no longer continue the struggle against the Allies. His last public appearance in Austria took place on 10 November, 1918, when he attended Mass at the imperial chapel at Schönbrunn, the elegant Habsburg palace in Vienna. Twenty-four hours later, faced with the threat of violent disorder, his Austrian cabinet gave him a draft document of abdication to sign. His wife, the Empress Zita, an Italian member of the Bourbon-Parma family, protested: 'A king can never abdicate: he can only be deposed. I would rather die with you here. Then Otto [their son] would succeed us, and if he were deposed there would always be enough Habsburgs left.'

What he actually signed subsequently was not strictly speaking an abdication, but rather a renunciation. As he told those subjects who remained loyal to him:

> Since my accession to the throne I have tried unceasingly to spare my peoples the horrors of the war, for the outbreak of which I bear no responsibility. I have never hesitated to restore constitutional life and I have opened the way for my peoples to their independent political development. Since I am filled, now as before, by unchangeable love for all my peoples, I will not interpose my person as an obstacle to their free evolution.

One of the last acts of the Habsburg emperor had been to name a new Prime Minister of Hungary, Count Mi'haly Károlyi, a rich landowner who had created a party in favour of Hungarian independence and democratic reforms. On 13 November, a delegation sent by Károlyi arrived, demanding that Karl I should give up the Hungarian crown as well. As with Austria, he renounced the title rather than abdicating, and made no promises regarding the future activities of his eldest son, Otto, the heir.

Four months later, the republic expelled Karl I and his family and expropriated them of their property. He settled for a time in Switzerland with his family, but twice made his way surreptitiously back to Hungary in unsuccessful attempts to reclaim his throne, in the second of which he and the Empress Zita were arrested. After this he acceded to British pressure that he should accept exile in order to avoid further stress and disturbance in his collapsed empire.

For his place of exile, Karl I chose Madeira, where his great-aunt, Empress Elizabeth I, had long ago sought solace from the grief over the suicide of her son and heir, Rudolf I. HMS *Cardiff* sailed from Sulina at nine o'clock on the morning of 7 November. She arrived in Gibraltar on 16 November, sailed again the following day, and sighted Porto Santo two days later, early on the morning of 19 November. Later that day, the logkeeper, still laconic, still inaccurate, noted:

'Ex-Emperor Karl of Hungary, the ex-Empress, Count and Countess Hunyadi and one attendant left the ship.'

In the interests of good naval housekeeping, the captain of HMS *Cardiff* asked for, and was given, a receipt by the manager of Reid's for the safe delivery of one former emperor and one former empress.

The exile of ex-Emperor Karl I proved even shorter than his brief, if tumultuous, reign. After leaving Reid's and settling in a modest house at the Monte, the summer resort of Madeiran residents two thousand feet above sea level, he died—aged only thirty-five—of a lung complaint in the year after his arrival. His remains are buried in a side chapel of the church of Our Lady of Monte. His widow, always a lover of Reid's, made two visits to the hotel in later years.

(later King Edward VIII for a short time before his Abdication), who looked in at Reid's on his way to South Africa and enjoyed the cocktail served to him so much that he persuaded a highly reluctant Fred Capitano, the Italian barman, to give him the recipe. Guests from other parts of the world ranged from a cross-section of Europe's Continental nobility to the Maharajah Gaekwar of Baroda, head of one of India's most important and enlightened princely states, and Austrian poet Rainer Maria Rilke, for a time secretary to the French sculptor Rodin whose best-known works include 'The Thinker', 'The Kiss' and 'The Burghers of Calais'.

*   *   *

It has been said that, if you want to make money, you should work with money. This proved to be a false adage in the case of the Reid brothers. Encouraged by their success as hoteliers, they decided to branch out into banking and commerce, two spheres in which they lacked the expertise they had acquired in the business of running successful hotels. Financial difficulties forced them in 1925 to sell the building that had made their family name internationally famous, and Reid's became the property of an English company, Reid's Palace Hotel (Madeira) Ltd. Despite the hotel's illustrious patronage, it became clear as the clouds of war began to gather in the second half of the 1930s that the building needed alterations, extensions and improvements if it was to maintain its position of eminence among the world's great hotels. This, of course, required fresh capital. Consequently, in 1937 Reid's Palace Hotel (Madeira) Ltd. went into voluntary liquidation but continued in business as Island Hotel (Madeira) Ltd. under its present owners, the Blandy family, who injected some £35,000 into the company.

Above: The offices of the Reid brothers' ill-fated banking venture, and one of the bank's cheques.

Below: John Paquot, manager of Reid's Hotel in 1933. *Photo: Museu Vicentes*

THE ONLY MAN WHO EVER TAUGHT ME ANYTHING

The Irish dramatist George Bernard Shaw arrived in Madeira on board the liner *Edinburgh Castle* on 30 December, 1924, for an extended holiday. He was sixty-eight. It was the year that had seen the staging of the last of his great plays, *Saint Joan*, and was to be followed a few months later by the award of the Nobel Prize for Literature. From the very start a deep shadow was cast over what should have been a happy occasion, for on his arrival GBS was greeted with the news that his great friend William Archer, the playwright and critic, had died after an operation for cancer.

In the mornings he worked and bathed amid what he described as 'unimaginable blossoms in mid-winter'. Grief over the loss of his close friend caused the rest of the day to drag. He sought to relieve his sadness by taking tango lessons from Max Rinder, the resident dancing instructor at Reid's, whose wife had undergone a similar, but successful, operation. Before leaving Reid's on 12 February, 1925, again on board the *Edinburgh Castle*, Shaw gave Max Rinder a signed photograph bearing the words: 'To the only man who ever taught me anything'.

Top: George Bernard Shaw ready for a swim during his stay at Reid's Hotel in 1924–25, and *below:* practising the tango under the watchful eye of the dancing instructor, Max Rinder.

QUEEN OF THE SKIES

Amy Johnson was already a legend when she arrived at Reid's for a spring holiday in March 1933. Three years earlier, still only in her mid-twenties, she had become the first woman to fly solo from Britain to Australia in her frail de Havilland Gipsy Moth aircraft *Jason*. In the course of the flight, which took 19-and-a-half days, she had to avoid mountains that were too high to fly over and cross shark-infested seas. In recognition of her feat, the *Daily Mail* of London awarded her a prize of £10,000, which was an enormous sum of money in those days. A year later, in the summer of 1931, she achieved further fame by flying from Britain to Tokyo in under nine days at the controls of a single-wing, single-engined de Havilland Puss Moth.

In July 1932, Amy Johnson had married another famous aviator of his time, Jim Mollison. A few months later, she set a new record time of 4 days 6 hours and 54 minutes for the flight from Lympne in England to Cape Town in South Africa, and a month later set a record of 7 days 7 hours and 5 minutes for the return journey. Princess Marie Louise, the favourite grand-daughter of Britain's Queen Victoria, arrived at Reid's on holiday, on the same day as the flyer. She was so intrigued with Amy Johnson's exploits, headline-making in what were still the comparatively early days of aviation, that she invited her to lunch.

During the war that followed seven years later, Amy Johnson served with the Air Transport Auxiliary, ferrying bombers to Britain from the United States. She disappeared while flying over the Thames Estuary on 5 January, 1941.

Top: Amy Johnson (Mrs Mollison) by the rock pool on her visit to Reid's Hotel in March 1933, and *below:* lunching with HRH Princess Marie Louise on the hotel balcony.

Dawn of a New Era

3

Dawn of a New Era

THE FIRST member of the Blandy family to set foot in Madeira was John Blandy, a quartermaster with General Beresford's forces which garrisoned the island in 1801 and again from 1807 to 1814. John Blandy, who was born in Dorchester, England, returned to his native country in 1810 to marry Janet Burden at St Andrew's Church in the central London district of Holborn. Twelve months later he returned to Madeira where he set up in business as a general merchant and—like William Reid—an exporter of Madeira wine.

Early records of the shipment of Madeira wine are obscure. However, the British nobleman, George, Duke of Clarence, imprisoned in the Tower of London in 1477, on being allowed to choose how he was to die is said to have opted for drowning in a butt of malmsey, and it is known that as early as 1485 Madeira wine formed part of a parish priest's stipend in England. By the middle of the sixteenth century it was being shipped to France and the Low Countries for 3,200 *reis* (75p) a pipe (105 gallons), and at the end of that century was mentioned twice in the Falstaff plays of William Shakespeare—*Henry IV* (parts I and II), *Henry V* and *The Merry Wives of Windsor*.

At one point, one of the characters, Mistress Quickly, the hostess of the tavern, observing the fat, comic figure of Sir John Falstaff approaching, shrieks: 'Yonder he comes: and that arrant malmsey-nose knave, Bardolph, with him.' Elsewhere Poins, one of Falstaff's companions, asks: 'Jack, how agrees the devil with thee about thy soul, that thou soldest him on Good Friday last for a cup of Madeira and a cold capon's leg?'

One the chief characteristics of Madeira wine, its agreeable 'burnt' taste, was discovered by accident. In the days of sailing ships, wine shipped to the New World and the Far East, but not sold, was found on its return to have changed. The two contributory factors were the rolling of the ship and, even more important, that the stored casks spent weeks, and often months, in the tropics and the temperature of the wine could rise to as high as 35°C. The voyage, along with fortification, was also found to prolong the life of the wine: a bottle of Madeira, once opened, will remain drinkable for months and the oldest vintage in Reid's cellars dates from 1826.

It became the custom to ship Madeira around the world as ballast to achieve these characteristics, and it was said that the wine ought really to cross the tropics twice before it was ready. The Napoleonic Wars around the end of the eighteenth century made it difficult to continue the practice because of shortage of shipping space. It was—as so often with the liquid pleasures of the table—a monk who came to the rescue by inventing *estufagem*, the process used today.

This simulates a voyage around the world by gradually bringing the temperature of the wine up to around 42°C over a period of five months, then allowing it to return to normal temperature in the sixth. It is less romantic than the old method, but more efficient. The amount of wine lost is only four per cent compared to ten per cent under the shipping method, a difference accounted for in part by the fact that sailors have been known to take a drink on the sly.

*　　*　　*

The export of wine continued to be the main business of John Blandy and his son, Charles Ridpath Blandy. With the arrival of coal-burning ships, however, John Burden Blandy, the third generation of the family, was not slow to see the opportunity to expand into new lines of business. He bought waterside storage space for coal, built lighters to carry coal, water barges to carry fresh water, and tugs to tow both lighters and barges out to the ships anchored in Funchal roads—and, in the process, became known locally by the affectionate nickname 'King Coal'. Wine, coal and shipping were therefore the three principal activities of the family which acquired control of Reid's in 1937.

New ownership led to the first substantial changes to the hotel since it had been first built nearly half a century earlier—the construction of the East Wing, which had barely been completed when the outbreak of the Second World War caused the hotel to be placed on a care-and-maintenance basis from 1940 until 1949, when one of the highlights in the long history of Reid's was a visit by Winston Churchill (see p. 67).

The board of Island Hotel (Madeira) Ltd. realised from the start the importance to the hotel's reputation of expert advice. Over the years they therefore co-opted the services of a number of distinguished figures from the hotel world, including Rudolph Richard, who had been managing director of the Connaught Hotel in London. He served the board from 1951 to 1973, and was succeeded by Richard Hargreaves, who had been responsible for co-ordinating contracts for the construction of the new Berkeley Hotel, again in London. An unexpected link between the two distinguished hotels designed by the architect George Somers Clarke—Shepheard's in Cairo and Reid's—was made in 1952 when, after the former had been destroyed in a disastrous fire, its general manager, Antonio Foerster, arrived in Funchal to take over as general manager of Reid's.

Once travelling had returned to something approaching pre-war normality, Reid's set in train a number of alterations and improvements which have continued ever since. In 1956 the cocktail bar was enlarged and the main restaurant extended and redecorated. Until then, from the time the hotel was built, the main restaurant had been on one level, the left-hand side, which contained the best tables, being known familiarly to guests as the 'House of Lords' because of the number of British peers who dined there, and what is now the middle section, under the

Top left: The pool restaurant.

Top right: The Villa Cliff restaurant.

Left: The stairway to the gardens, by the Churchill suite.

Photos: Andreas von Einsiedel

Top left: Funchal bay can be glimpsed through the trees.

Top right: Colour and luxuriance in the flower borders. *Photo: Andreas von Einsiedel*

Right: The gardens run right to the edge of the cliff. *Photo: Andreas von Einsiedel*

Facing page left: Protea, with its exotic blooms. *Photo: Alexes Weaver*

Facing page right: The 'engraved' cactus – easier to write on than the bark of a tree!

Top left: The bar overlooking the gardens.

Top right: The bridge room.

Right: The Churchill suite, where Winston Churchill stayed in 1950.

Photos: Andreas von Einsiedel

Madeira wine remains one of the most important elements in the island's economy. Madeira is a versatile as well as a durable wine that can serve as an accompaniment to most stages of a meal. Sercial, the driest wine with a full-bodied, 'nutty' tang, should be served chilled as an aperitif; Verdelho, medium dry with a subtle toasted aroma, may also be served slightly chilled, with the soup; Bual, medium rich with an underlying acidity and a full, honeyed taste, is ideal with dessert or cheese, and Malmsey, richest of the four wines, is usually served with coffee at the end of a meal.

John Blandy established his lodges a hundred and fifty years ago next door to a former Franciscan monastery in the centre of Funchal, and was one of the founder members when a number of producers combined to form the Madeira Wine Company. The company, in which the Blandy family are today joint major shareholders, still operates near the sixteenth-century former monastery and sells between 1.2 and 1.4 million litres of Madeira wine—roughly half and half in bottle and in bulk—all over the world. The importance of wine to the island's prosperity is celebrated each year with a gala at Reid's.

A visit to the wine lodges to watch a film, see the actual wine-making process and sample the end product is a popular way of passing an hour with most visitors to Funchal. They can, of course, also buy any of the four wines that take their fancy. The oldest vintage available for sale dates from 1863. It is priced at just over £150 a bottle.

Menu for the Madeira wine gala night in February 1965.

A WHALE OF A TIME

The opening scenes of *Moby Dick*, the film of Herman Melville's epic nineteenth-century novel about the pursuit by Captain Ahab of a great white whale, were filmed at Youghal in Southern Ireland where all signs of modernity were stripped from the street fronting the harbour and the houses were repainted to look like New England clapboard. Afterwards, John Huston, the legendary Hollywood director, set out with his star, Gregory Peck, for Madeira to shoot some of the preliminary whale-hunting scenes. Madeira had been chosen because, with the Azores, it was one of the two places in the world at that time where whalers rowed up to their quarry in open boats and plunged their harpoons in by hand rather than firing them from the safety of a ship's deck.

Huston and Gregory Peck, who stayed at Reid's, went on several whaling expeditions. After one of them, Huston—who by and large preferred to hunt, shoot and fish than do anything else—recalled enthusiastically: 'In a single day we killed twenty whales, killed them the old way. This can be incredibly exciting. Unless you've harpooned a.whale in rough seas you haven't really hunted.'

After Madeira, some scenes were shot in a tank at Shepperton Studios outside London before the cast moved to Fishguard in South Wales. Although the Madeira scenes were authentic, several model whales—ninety feet long and made of steel and wood, covered with latex—were constructed at a cost of around £15,000 each to play the 'part' of Moby Dick in the rest of the film. Some simply sank. Finally, a successful model was made that would submerge and surface according to the speed at which it was being towed by a tug. However, shooting of the film was dogged by bad weather and two of these models were lost when the two-inch nylon towlines snapped in heavy seas. The second of them drifted out to sea, where it was reported by a liner as a danger to shipping, and was eventually found on a beach in Holland, some six hundred miles away.

As a result of this latest disaster, shooting was transferred to the Canary Islands where yet another model whale was constructed. The cast and crew then returned to London where the final death scene was filmed in an 80,000-gallon tank. It involved Captain Ahab being strapped to the mid-section of the whale, which was rotated on a drum so that with each revolution Gregory Peck, now supposedly dead, reappeared more and more firmly attached to his mortal enemy by a tangle of harpoon lines.

Later he recalled: 'The wind machines were roaring and I was half-drowned by torrents of water. John Huston said: "I want you with your eyes staring open as you come slowly out of the sea—with your dead hand beckoning your crew to their doom." What I didn't know was that the winch they were using to rotate the section I was tied to was hand-operated and that when they first tried it out it had stuck. I could really have come up dead, which I think would have secretly pleased John, providing a last touch of realism.'

Moby Dick, beset by bad weather and problems with its model whale, took more than twice as long to make as had been planned. Its cost of £1.7 million was also double the original budget. Despite that, it was not a critical success. John Huston, who often described it as his favourite film, complained that the critics' disapproval—and, in particular, their hostility to Gregory Peck's interpretation of the role of Captain Ahab—arose from a failure to understand the theme of *Moby Dick*: 'The whole thing is a blasphemy. Melville hated God! I never saw Captain Ahab as a ranting madman, and Peck furnished a kind of nobility, a heroic stature—but his performance didn't coincide with critics' ideas about Ahab.'

Left: John Huston, director of the film *Moby Dick*.

Below: Gregory Peck as Captain Ahab clings to the back of the white whale, striking at it with his harpoon. Scene from the film *Moby Dick*.

high ceiling, the 'House of Commons'. As part of the improvements to the main restaurant a raised section was now built on the right.

The next eight years saw a process of continuous modernisation—without in any way affecting the smooth tenor of the hotel's life—which included the installation of private bathrooms throughout the main building and the redecoration and refurnishing of all the bedrooms, sitting-rooms and lounges existing at that time. No sooner had this work been completed than another project began—construction of the Garden Wing and Grill Room, as well as two sea-water swimming pools, both heated, in the garden. These replaced two buildings which the more elderly guests of Reid's still remember with affection—the Bungalow, where lunch was prepared in the summer months, and the Pavilion, where it was served. The Garden Wing was completed at three o'clock on the morning of 24 December, 1967, and all its rooms were occupied that night. Later improvements included linking the hotel draining system to that of Funchal, greater refrigeration capacity and the installation of air conditioning.

In the summer of 1990 Reid's closed down to make further changes in preparation for the centenary year which lay twelve months ahead. Improvements were made to the support installations, including boilers; the cocktail bar was extended and its décor changed; the sixth-floor Grill Room was redecorated, enhanced with original Picasso line-drawings and given a less prosaic name, Les Faunes; six new suites were constructed beyond it; a new restaurant, the Villa Cliff, specialising in Portuguese and Madeiran cuisine, was opened in the grounds; additional marble was laid upon the pillars of the main restaurant to give the room even greater elegance—and the centre of the main-restaurant ceiling was repainted.

This ceiling had been at the centre of a schism among the regular guests some years before, when the air conditioning was being installed. For decades the cen-

Reid's is quite a small hotel compared to some of the towering monstrosities that have been built elsewhere to cater for the mass tourist market—152 rooms with sea view and balcony, 21 suites with sea view, balcony or terrace.

Impeccable service is ensured by employing staff totalling around 350, at least one for every guest at most periods of the year: tradition of service follows automatically from the fact that most of the staff who join the hotel look upon it as a job for life. At any given time, it is possible to find up to ten members of the staff who have been with the company for a quarter of a century at least; some, like Joseph, the hall porter, who had served hotel guests in various capacities for more than fifty years before his retirement.

tral panel had been a russet colour with details picked out in gold, but in order to accommodate the air conditioning it was suggested that a false ceiling should be put in, which would have covered the familiar panel. However, Richard Blandy then discovered that in the matter of the ceiling a love-hate relationship existed among guests, who tend to look upon Reid's as a home from home and take a proprietary interest in any alterations that the owners might envisage.

'Our regular guests come out at the same time year after year and ask for the same rooms and the same tables,' he explained. 'When they heard that we proposed to cover the central panel they divided into two rival groups. One group said they would never stay at the hotel again if the panel were hidden, the other that they would never stay at the hotel again if not.'

In the end it was decided to solve the problem of the air conditioning in some other way and to leave the ceiling as it was. In 1990, however, when the russet panel was painted over to represent the clouds that gather most days over the tall hills above Funchal Bay, there was no outcry among the guests at all. They appear to have found the change rather pleasing to the eye.

A drawing by Picasso decorates the menu of the newly redecorated gourmet restaurant on the sixth floor, Les Faunes. The new Villa Cliff restaurant in the hotel grounds, illustrated on the menu, specialises in local and national dishes.

Mussolini, the Italian dictator, once made the point: 'You can create a successful coup with the army or without the army, but never against the army.' During the summer of 1958, in the early days of his final assault on the regime of General Fulgencio Batista Zaldívar, the dictator who had ruled Cuba since 1940, Dr Fidel Castro explained to a visiting American journalist: 'We are proving Mussolini wrong. We are winning here against the army.' It was not a hollow boast, although he commanded a force of only two hundred and thirty men at the time.

As the year drew to a close, Castro—the ranks of his revolutionary army by then increased through a mass of supporters who had rallied to his cause—was poised for the victory that would result in the first Communist state in the Western Hemisphere, only ninety miles from the nearest point on the mainland of the United States, and would lead to the fiasco of the Bay of Pigs invasion by US forces and the subsequent Cuban missile crisis which brought the world as close to nuclear war as it has yet been.

The armed forces of Batista were in disarray, with few of them having stomach for further action against the revolutionaries and one group of senior officers putting forward secret proposals for a peace settlement. It was increasingly clear that the people, in cities as well as the countryside, had lost faith in the man who had ruled them for the better part of two decades. The legendary Argentine guerrilla Che Guevara—later gunned down in Bolivia where he had sought new battles because 'other hills of the world demand the aid of my modest efforts'—captured the regional capital of Santa Clara on 30 December.

Shortly after midnight on New Year's Eve, General Batista, his family and his closest associates drove to Camp Columbia airfield in north-western Havana and boarded a plane bound for Cuba's Caribbean neigh-

bour, the Dominican Republic. The republic was considered too close to Cuba for comfort and the United States made it clear that they were opposed to the general settling permanently in Florida, where he had a home. Therefore, like ex-Emperor Karl and ex-Empress Zita of Austria forty years earlier, the deposed dictator decided to settle for Reid's.

He arrived with a retinue that included his wife, five children, his chief of staff, a former captain of Cuban military intelligence, two other officers, several bodyguards and two maids, and took over the whole third floor of the hotel at a cost estimated at £750 a week, which was an enormous sum of money in those days. The world wondered, naturally, how he could afford it when, in addition, during term time, he had to support a son at college in the United States and two other sons at a finishing school in Switzerland.

The official answer was that the General had been able to cash in life assurance policies he had bought in the United States to ensure his children's education. Unofficial sources took the view that he was simply tapping a contingency fund—one guess, which appeared in print, put it as high as £100 million—that he had salted away for just such an emergency.

Marc Burca, the son of Reid's manager at the time, struck up a firm friendship with Carlos, one of the two younger Batista boys, who was about his own age. 'We used to go to Dr Bardoso's school, the main school in Madeira, together by taxi with an armed bodyguard,' he explained. 'As his best friend, I also used to go up to the third floor to play with him. It was very James Bondish. There were always armed bodyguards with shoulder holsters hanging about, usually three or four on duty at a time. I don't know why, but they seemed to congregate near the third-floor room that had been equipped with a short-wave radio. The Batistas always used taxis with the same drivers. If we went on a picnic there would be a fleet of them, like a presidential convoy, because all the guards came as well.

'The general was certainly the most talked-about of Reid's guests while he was there, much more than someone like, say, Rab Butler, the British Home Secretary, who was a regular visitor in those days. I remember that the general always smoked cigars—you could tell where he had been by a whiff of cigar smoke in the air—but my chief recollection is probably very different from those painted by history. I look back on him as an incredibly generous man. Whenever we went on picnics he would seek out poor people and give them gifts and money.'

The sad death of Carlos from leukaemia at the age of eighteen, and the departure of the general to live in Lisbon, did not sever Mr Burca's friendship with the Batistas: 'I had dinner with the general and his family at the Grosvenor House Hotel in London just a few days before he died and I'm still vaguely in touch with Roberto, his second son. We had lunch together a couple of years ago, but there's not a lot of opportunity to see him as he lives part of the year in Madrid and the other part in Miami.'

Left: General Batista and his wife during their stay at Reid's Hotel.
Photo: Museu Vicentes

Above: Richard and Marc Burca, sons of Reid's manager, Jean Burca, with Carlos Batista, dressed for a fancy-dress carnival.
Photo: Museu Vicentes

DID DR ADAMS GET AWAY WITH MURDER?

The trouble with Dr John Bodkin Adams was that his elderly women patients kept leaving him a little something in their wills and, soon afterwards, dying. After the demise of Mrs Edith Morrell, aged 81, police inquiries revealed no fewer than one hundred and thirty-two wills that named the chubby Irish doctor from County Antrim as a beneficiary.

On 26 November, 1956, Detective Inspector Herbert Hannam called on Dr Adams at his Sussex home with the news that the police were investigating Mrs Morrell's death. Dr Adams took an optimistic view of the situation. 'Easing the passing of a dying person is not all that wicked,' he explained. 'She wanted to die. That cannot be murder. It is impossible to accuse a doctor.'

Three weeks later, Hannam proved him wrong. He arrested Dr Adams and charged him with Mrs Morrell's murder. The alleged motive? That she was threatening to change her will and remove the name of the doctor as a beneficiary. Dr Adams replied: 'I did not think you could prove murder. She was dying in any event.' The outcome was one of the most dramatic murder trials of the century—and later a threat by Dr Adams to sue a blameless Reid's for invasion of his privacy.

The trial was characterised by an element of hostility between the judge and the then Attorney-General, Sir Reginald Manningham-Buller, whose aggressive personality had resulted in his enjoying the nickname Sir Bullying Manner. The judge, who took the view that the prosecution was pitching its case too high, refused to allow admission of evidence about other elderly women patients who had died after naming the doctor in their wills. The prosecution's case was also seriously undermined when the defence produced medical evidence that, at a time when she was alleged to have been in a coma, Mrs Morrell had actually been sitting up in bed eating partridge with celery and drinking brandy and soda. After a friendly summing up, Dr Adams was acquitted—and decided later to celebrate with a holiday in Madeira.

He arrived at Reid's with a woman companion, who showed every sign of being in excellent health, but felt his holiday had been marred when an enterprising Funchal photographer, who realised who he was, took a picture of him. Dr Adams blamed the hotel. His threat to take legal action evaporated, however, when he was persuaded that the photographer had no connection with the hotel and, while the name of Adams might be famous—or notorious—in Britain, the staff at Reid's had never heard of him.

Did Dr Adams get away with murder? There is no doubt that he was a compulsive legacy-hunter. At the time of his trial—and today—many believe that he was one of the great mass-murderers of history, winning the confidence of rich old ladies, prescribing morphia and heroin for their ailments and finally giving them an overdose once he was sure of a mention in their will. When he died in 1983, at the age of 84, *The Times* newspaper described him as 'the classic enigma in the history of mass killing'.

In his own will, Dr Adams left £402,970. It was a lot of money for a local doctor who had been retired for the better part of twenty years.

Dr John Bodkin Adams, acquitted of the murder of Mrs Edith Morrell, who celebrated his freedom with a holiday at Reid's Hotel.

BLACK CHRISTMAS

The eldest of the thirty-two children on board the 20,000-ton cruise liner *Lakonia* were singing carols in one of the ship's lounges. Nearby, in the gaily-lit ball-room, bright with Christmas decorations, the majority of the adult passengers, many in fancy dress, were enjoying themselves at the Tramps' Ball. Some of the more elderly had already retired for the night.

The ball was in full swing when the first traces of smoke began to seep into the room through the ventilators. By midnight the liner was ablaze from stem to stern, nearly two hundred miles north of Madeira. As the minutes of the new day—23 December, 1963—ticked away, the *Lakonia's* wireless operator sent the last of several SOS messages and added: 'I cannot stay any more in the wireless cabin. We are leaving the ship. Please help immediately.'

The liner, with 1,036 passengers and crew, had left Southampton three days earlier on an eleven-day sun-shine cruise that had been advertised, ironically in the light of events, as 'a holiday with all the risks removed' and—in words that were to prove prophetic in a more tragic sense than the tour company intended—as 'a holiday you will remember, and talk about, for the rest of your life'. However, a number of the passengers had not booked for the cruise but planned to leave the *Lakonia* at its first port of call, Funchal. They included more than sixty guests who intended to celebrate Christmas at Reid's; Richard Blandy and his two younger brothers, and Richard Burca, the elder son of Reid's manager at the time, Jean Burca, all of whom were returning from school in Britain to spend their holidays in Madeira; Mrs Elisabeth Burca's mother; and Malcolm Flux, son of the manager of Blandy's Travel Agency.

It was to be a black Christmas. The first newspaper reports were not encouraging. First Lieutenant Kenneth Hoffman, the pilot of a US Air Force plane which dropped life-rafts to passengers and crew in the water, reported that he first sighted the liner when he broke through cloud fifteen miles away. 'It was like a burning building,' he said. First Lieutenant Larry Dishon, a member of the crew of another US Air Force plane, said: 'I thought I was having a bad dream. The people were helpless in the water. A lot of them waved to us. I saw a little child of about two or three years of age in a life-jacket with nobody near him.' The *Lakonia*, listing to starboard, had apparently had its sides blown open by a boiler explosion, and Christmas presents were among the debris that littered the water around the blazing vessel.

As the hours passed, a number of ships arrived at the scene to pick up survivors and bodies—the British liner *Stratheden*, which had hospital facilities, the British aircraft carrier *Centaur*, diverted by the Admiralty from a voyage to the Far East, the Argentine liner *Salta*, the British steamer *Montcalm*, which was first on the scene and reported that, while the water was warm enough for survival, rescue work was difficult because of the high seas; and the Pakistani steamer *Mehdi*.

News of the disaster first reached Madeira around two o'clock on the morning of 23 December. 'We went straight down to see Graham Blandy (uncle of the present owners of Reid's), who was the agent for the ship,' said Mrs Burca. Naturally, in view of the short time that had elapsed, there was nothing further he could add to what they knew already. Mr and Mrs Burca went back to Reid's to spend a sleepless night.

On Christmas Eve, the Argentine liner *Salta* arrived in Funchal Bay with more than four hundred survivors and a number of bodies. The local vicar identified Richard Burca as one of the bodies laid out in the Funchal mortuary, but the identification proved false. In the meantime, Mr and Mrs Burca had begun sending telegrams to all the ships known to have taken part in

The cruise liner *Lakonia* in flames, seen from the air, during the disaster of Christmas 1963.
Photo: Associated Press

the rescue operation and to submarines reported still to be searching in the area in the hope of finding further survivors. The replies came back: 'No trace of anyone named Richard Burca.'

Amid the fears, despondency and gloom, preparations still had to continue for the Christmas night celebrations, a carnival occasion at Reid's, to which had been added an additional burden: the hotel, already booked fully for the holiday, had been asked to accommodate a hundred of the survivors of the tragedy, who had just arrived. 'We enlisted the help of the Portuguese army, who provided us with beds and blankets,' said Mr Burca. 'We even had survivors sleeping in the billiards room.' His wife recalls that the survivors 'were in a terrible state of shock and had no clothes. Many of them also had serious neck injuries caused by their life-jackets when they jumped into the sea from the blazing ship.'

Marc Burca, their younger son, who is now the former owner, chairman and editor of the prestigious *Boardroom* business magazine in London, was twelve years old at the time. 'I remember that Christmas chiefly because my brother was missing and we had no news of him. The bathing boys down at the Reid's pool were all very optimistic. Richard had a lot of life-saving medallions and was a life-saving instructor, and they said: "If anyone is going to be saved, it's Richard. He'll survive anything if he can get into the water." But all the telegrams that came back were negative.'

Marc Burca remembers that Christmas night as a time when there were empty seats at tables where there should have been guests—several who had planned to spend the holiday at Reid's had been drowned—and what is normally a gay occasion was overwhelmed with sorrow and fear of what the news might be. 'At our table there was a boy of about nine named Christopher—I can't remember his other name—who used to come out with his family every year. His mother was with him, but his father was missing. On Christmas night, when we were all trying hard to be jolly on what was basically a sad evening, the news arrived that his father had perished. He took it very well, but I think he was probably too young to understand the significance of what had happened.'

The grief and fears that had marred Christmas up to that point were forgotten by the Blandy and Burca families on Boxing Day. 'At last we had some news—and, thank God, the Blandy boys, Richard and my mother were all safe,' said Mrs Burca. 'They had been rescued and taken to Casablanca.' The town turned out to greet them when they finally arrived in Funchal on a ship from Lisbon, and Richard Burca, fifteen at the time, later received a bravery award from his English school, Milton Abbey, for his efforts to try to save the lives of others in the water.

In all, ninety passengers, mostly British, and thirty-one members of the *Lakonia's* crew died on that tragic night when 'a holiday you will remember, and talk about, for the rest of your life' turned into a nightmare that all those who were involved in and survived would never be able to forget.

Reid's Hotel menu for the tragic Christmas dinner of 1963. Empty seats at the tables were a constant reminder of those who had been drowned.

THE CURSE OF THE GRIMALDIS

The visit to Reid's by ex-King Umberto, last of Italy's royal rulers, coincided with that of a certain countess who had married into the widely-scattered Grimaldi family.

She was desperately anxious to meet the former king, but the hotel staff took the view that she was simply a member of American café society who had happened to marry into a branch of European nobility and was therefore not an entirely suitable person—purely in terms of social standing—to be introduced to the ruler who had abdicated, like his father before him, in May 1946. Various stratagems were employed to ensure that the countess's wishes were frustrated.

In the end she had her modest revenge. On the night before her holiday was to end, she stalked the hotel corridors, collected all the guests' shoes that had been left out for cleaning and piled them in a heap on the lawn.

Ex-King Umberto of Italy at Reid's Hotel in January 1965. *Photo: Museu Vicentes*

Journey to the Sun

Ceia do Carnaval
na Madeira

REID'S HOTEL
MADEIRA

4

Journey to the Sun

THE Scottish author Robert Louis Stevenson once made the much-quoted observation that 'to travel hopefully is a better thing than to arrive'. Before Funchal airport opened in 1964, guests escaping to Reid's from the damp, cold winters of Northern Europe could be forgiven if they often came to the conclusion that the opposite were true. Sea-sickness has long enjoyed a deserved reputation as the worst scourge of the sea voyager, a reputation reflected in the elaborate antidotes—largely unsuccessful—for *mal de mer* which have been suggested down the centuries. They have included a belladonna plaster on the stomach, bismuth, opium, Worcester sauce, mustard leaves, caviar, chewing gum, a slice of fat pork fried with garlic, soup with cayenne pepper, tomato sauce, a draught of sea water, sips of vinegar and water, trinitrin and cocaine, arrowroot and wine, soda, cannabis, toast, a spinal ice-bag, mustard pickles and small doses of tincture of iodine.

In their guide *Madeira*, the Reid brothers sought,

understandably, to reassure 'poor' sailors about the possible rigours of the voyage by a quotation from the authoritative *British Medical Journal*: 'The invalid need not dread this voyage. Sea-sickness is most rarely other than slight and transient, and the whole trip is positively beneficial and without fatigue.' Anyone who did not take kindly to the sea, and had just crossed the Bay of Biscay in a winter gale, would have found this view unduly optimistic, and welcomed with relief the sight of the green Madeiran hills bathed in sunlight.

At the time the hotel opened, Madeira was linked with Northern Europe by several shipping lines. There were services from Southampton, Liverpool, London and Hamburg, while anyone in fear of the Bay of Biscay's reputation could travel overland to Lisbon and board a steamer there. Typical fares for the outward voyage from Northern Europe at the time, including rail fares to and from London, were, first class 13 guineas (£13.65); second class 8 guineas (£8.40); third

Advertisement for a shipping line with weekly sailings to Madeira, from *A Handy Guide to Madeira* by Jones (1901).

class 6 guineas (£6.30). The Woerman Line offered a return fare of £16 on its monthly service from Hamburg, and both the African Steam Ship Company and British and African Company charged £15 return on their fortnightly sailings from Liverpool.

Arriving in Funchal at the end of a voyage lasting less than four days was—despite the gloomy opinion of Robert Louis Stevenson—a colourful and exciting experience. As soon as a liner appeared and prepared to anchor in Funchal Bay, an armada of small boats set out from the shore to greet it. With them they brought mixed cargoes of humanity—small boys, who were skilful swimmers and dived to retrieve coins thrown into the sea by passengers . . . vendors waiting to board the vessel at the first opportunity and set out on the decks their stocks of embroidery, basket-work, linen, straw hats, jewellery of silver and gold, and other goods . . . excursion agents looking for business.

There still remained, of course, the matter of getting ashore, which could be a somewhat daunting experience for elderly guests if an Atlantic swell were running. Once ferried to Reid's own landing-stage by small boat, guests faced the long climb up the steps of the garden to the hotel above. This situation continued until the late 1920s when, after the hotel had passed out of Reid family ownership, the new company appointed one of the many remarkable managers who have contributed to the success of Reid's down the years.

Luigi Gandolfo, an Italian who had served his apprenticeship at the old Cecil Hotel in London, arrived in Madeira via the Palace Hotel in Montreux and the Westminster in Paris. It was he who first decided to do something about what the Reid brothers had described as 'the great want of Funchal'—bathing. At the time the facilities were much as they had been when the hotel first opened, a choice between the sea or the small rock pool, and, while female guests enjoyed the use of three cabins for changing, men had to make do with a cave. During Luigi Gandolfo's regime, a new row of

58

The British statesman David Lloyd George being helped ashore at Reid's landing stage when he arrived with his family in 1925 for their second visit. At dinner one night, a guest at the same table had the misfortune to bite her tongue. On recovering from the pain, she asked the former British Prime Minister, who had made his initial political reputation as a fiery Radical and Welsh Nationalist: 'Have you ever bitten your tongue?' 'Frequently,' he answered, 'but not soon enough.' *Photo: Museu Vicentes*

In the late 1950s and early 1960s, two of the favourite figures for British gossip columnists were Sir Bernard and Lady Docker. Sir Bernard, an indulgent husband, was a director of a score or so of companies, including being chairman of the firm that made Daimler motor cars. Much was made of the fact that, as a result, thrice-married Lady Docker had use of a special gold-plated model with zebra-patterned seats.

It was not so much this display of ostentation that attracted the newspapers' attention as Lady Docker's erratic behaviour. In a fit of pique because her son by a previous marriage, Lance Reventlow, had not been invited to the christening of Prince Albert, the heir to the throne of Monaco, Lady Docker tore up a paper Monagasque flag. Prince Rainier promptly banned the Dockers from the principality, which, under the terms of a treaty with France, resulted in their also being banned from the entire French Riviera.

This proved inconvenient as the Riviera had been one of Sir Bernard's favourite cruising grounds in his luxurious yacht, the *Shemara*. A flirtation with Italy proved brief when Lady Docker found herself facing possible legal charges for abusing a Customs officer. The Dockers then turned their attention to Madeira where, although they lived aboard the *Shemara*, they became regular visitors to Reid's to drink and dine.

Lady Docker was fond of saying that she had an especially soft spot for hoteliers—'My first boyfriend was the manager of the Queen's Hotel in Birmingham, who committed suicide when I fell in love with somebody else'—and one Christmas she gave a tape-recorder to Richard and Marc Burca, the two sons of the manager of Reid's. Unfortunately, when they switched it on, a voice on the cassette said: 'Good morning, your ladyship. This is your butler. I and the staff wish you a happy Christmas and hope you will like our present.' The two Burca boys were placed in the embarrassing position of having to return the cassette with the explanation: 'There's a message on it for you, Lady Docker.'

Sir Bernard and Lady Docker in 1959, at the height of their fame.

cabins was built with a terrace, where drinking Madeira wine or Bovril became the popular way of relaxing after a swim; a lift was also installed, a benefit both to bathers and new guests arriving at the hotel landing-stage.

By this time the Union and Castle Lines, which had initially had separate services sailing from Southampton to Madeira in alternate weeks, had been amalgamated for a quarter of a century as the Union-Castle Line, a name synonymous with voyages both to Madeira and South Africa, and the eminence of Reid's had ensured a tradition that its guests had priority when the time came for disembarkation from liners anchored in Funchal Bay. At around the moment when the order 'Reid's visitors will disembark first, please' was being sounded, Luigi Gandolfo would make his way down to the landing-stage to receive them in person in an impressive ceremony when the hotel pinnace, with 'Reid's Palace Hotel' emblazoned on its side, ultimately arrived. One regular guest at the time recalled later; 'This incredible man impressed me to the point of awe. He ran his hotel as impeccably as he was turned out. Tall, slim, with a head of beautifully groomed white hair and a white moustache, he was always immaculately dressed in a white suit and always wore a buttonhole. He would greet each of his guests, bowing over their hands as if they were the only people he ever wished to see . . .'

He also doubled as the Italian consul, and when an Italian liner arrived in the bay would abandon temporarily his hotel duties and visit it garbed in all his consular finery, including a cocked hat. Legend has it that, in the course of one such visit, he suffered the misfortune of falling out of Reid's pinnace and having to be rescued from a potentially watery grave. Yet it is said that, such was his presence, he retained his dignity intact as he was hauled dripping from the Atlantic.

His own quarters were in the annexe, the Villa Victoria, where he interviewed potential staff and, after explaining what their duties would be, admonished them, as a good hotelier should: 'See all, hear all—and, *hush*, not a word.' José Fernandes, who joined the hotel staff as a page-boy at this time and later became a legendary hall porter for whom there were no problems, only solutions, recalls the man who gave him his first job in the hotel as 'firm, but fair'. Luigi Gandolfo could also dispense discipline with humour. Later, when Reid's was closed and placed on a care-and-maintenance basis from 1940 to 1949 because of the Second World War, he served as *maître d'hôtel* at the Savoy Hotel in London. One day he saw a waiter, thinking himself unobserved and clearly feeling the pinch of food rationing, slip a small chicken into his pocket. He pursued the miscreant into the kitchen and, observing politely: 'You've forgotten the sauce, allow me', emptied the contents of a sauce-boat into the offending waiter's pocket.

The British author and art critic Sir Sacheverell Sitwell stayed at Reid's in the autumn of 1953 when he was gathering material for his travel book *Portugal and Madeira*, published the following year. In it he described the magical experience of arriving at Funchal by liner in the early hours of the morning:

> . . . the whole town glittered before us . . . climbing up from sea level with lamplit roads zigzagging up into the hills . . . From nowhere an armada of little boats came out just as we cast anchor. Each boat carried a naphtha flare, and had for occupants a rower and a small boy to dive for pennies . . . Funchal was no longer a port. The armada or regatta of little rowing boats at half past one in the morning had some hint in it of arriving in Venice at the height of the Carnival.

In the immediate years after the Second World War, an attempt was made to spare voyagers from Britain the often unpleasant crossing of the Bay of Biscay, and to reduce the time it took to reach Madeira, by the

Guests arriving at Reid's Hotel steps in the 1930s.

Flying-boat at Madeira in March 1949.

The writer and art critic Sacheverell Sitwell, who visited Reid's in 1953, gathering material for his book *Portugal and Madeira*. *Photo by Baron: Camera Press*

introduction of a flying-boat service between Southampton and Funchal. With Britain facing severe bal-
ance-of-payments problems in the aftermath of the
war, it was a difficult period for the tourist industry.
British nationals were restricted to an annual travel
allowance of £25 (£15 for children under twelve years
of age). However, Aquila Airways, who operated the
flying-boat service, assured potential travellers in their
1951 *Guide* that it was still possible to take a two-week
holiday in Madeira without being haunted towards the
end by the thought: I wonder if my currency will last.
'Nothing,' they pointed out, 'could be more infuriating
than to have to spend the last two or three days virtually
confined to the hotel (with the bar out of bounds)
owing to lack of funds.'

Nobody, they asserted, need face such problems in
Madeira where . . .

hotel accommodation ranges from 16s. 3d. (81½p)
a day inclusive—and please remember that we are
talking not of a small *pension*, but of a genuine
hotel, where the rooms are comfortable and the
rooms are good . . . Even if you prefer one of the
larger hotels, taking the figure of £1. 5s. (£1.25) a
day, plus ten per cent service charge, £8. 10s.
(£8.50) still remains after paying the bill at the end
of a twelve-day holiday. With the possible excep-
tion of Spain, there are few, if any, comparable
resorts where the rates for first-class hotels are so
low. Particular attention should also be paid to the
special concessions enjoyed by Reid's and the
New Avenue Hotels whereby only £1. 5s. (£1.25) a
day (£1. 2s. 6d., or £1.12½ in summer), plus the
ten per cent service charge, need be paid in foreign
currency, the balance of the hotel account being
payable in sterling.

For those so inclined, there is, therefore, ample
scope for Bacchanalian activity. No comment is
necessary on the wines except to say that most

HRH the Duke of Kent on the hotel balcony after being welcomed
by the manager, Luigi Gandolfo, in January 1934.

Opposite: Prince Arthur and Princess Alexandra of Connaught
transferring from a liner to the small boat which would put them
ashore at Reid's landing-stage. *Photo: Museu Vicentes*

DID THE PRINCE RESCUE THE GRAND DUCHESS?

In the first half of 1918, when he was serving with considerable distinction on the Western Front, Prince Arthur of Connaught received a curt telegram from his uncle, Britain's King George V. It read: 'Please come home as soon as possible as I want to see you and you had better bring your things with you.'

The king had decided to present a field-marshal's baton to Emperor Yoshihito of Japan, a gift designed to quell his growing doubts about whether the Allies were capable of winning the First World War, and Prince Arthur had been chosen as somebody of suitable rank and distinction to present the gift. The prince sailed for Japan in the British naval vessel HMS *Suffolk*, made the planned presentation—and then disappeared.

Ostensibly, he and his party had taken a few days' leave. Their whereabouts and what they were doing were surrounded with so much secrecy, however, that Sir Conynham Greene, a British diplomat in Tokyo, sent a telegraphed report to London about a conversation that had taken place between Prince Arthur and the Japanese Prime Minister. It said in part: 'His Excellency added it was evident that in despatching Prince Arthur the King had something more in mind than the ceremonial of handing over a field-marshal's baton.'

The odd disappearance of the prince has given rise to speculation that, before the supposed massacre of the Tsar's entire family in the middle of July 1918 by the Soviet revolutionaries, one of his four daughters, the Grand Duchess Tatiana, escaped, was flown—with the aid of fuelling stops in friendly territory—to the Pacific coast and was there rescued by a Japanese naval vessel.

It has been suggested that Tatiana made her way by sea to the west coast of Canada, crossed Canada by rail and then sailed for London in the liner *Corsican*. On a voyage that ended in the Thames on 8 August, 1918, the liner's cabin 14 was occupied by the wife of Richard Meinertzhagen, head of one of Britain's intelligence services, and cabin 13 by a mysterious Canadian masseuse, aged twenty-two and named Marguerite Lindsay.

When the ship docked in London, she gave her address as a Canadian bank—and vanished. Tsar-watchers have never been able to find any subsequent trace of her or, in fact, of anyone of that name having been born in Canada or anywhere else at the appropriate time.

visitors are surprised at the wide variety available. There is a very good local brand of bottled beer, and Portuguese liqueurs are well worth trying. English cigarettes are on sale, ranging from 1s. (5p) for twenty . . . and a number of brands of pipe tobacco can be obtained at 1s. 3d. (7½p) an ounce.

These figures, then, will tell you what you want to know. Your question is: 'Can I spend twelve days in Madeira and still keep well within my £25 travel allowance?' Our answer—which we hope we have proved in the preceding paragraphs—is 'You most certainly can.'

It was the weather rather than shortages of foreign currency that eventually killed off the flying-boat service. The heavy swell that tends to run in Funchal Bay often made it impossible for flying-boats to land, and there were similar difficulties, largely resulting from poor visibility, at Southampton. Winston Churchill, forced by political events to cut short a holiday at Reid's at the beginning of 1950 and make a hurried journey home by flying-boat, wrote to his wife Clementine, who had stayed on at the hotel for a few extra days: 'We were lucky yesterday with fog, which obligingly lifted for half an hour.' Although the flight had been 'most comfortable', he recommended to his wife that it was better to return by sea.

New aquatic horrors awaited in 1961 when the airport on the neighbouring island of Porto Santo opened three years before Madeira's. For Reid's guests it meant a sea journey of almost forty miles to Funchal, an experience which often left them half-wishing that Zarco's sailors had been right in their prediction that they were about to find relief by sailing off the edge of an unstable world. 'They made the trip in flat-bottomed boats,' recalled Mrs Elisabeth Burca, the wife of Jean Burca, Reid's manager at the time. 'We used to receive some very green guests in those days.'

Today all has changed. Direct flights from London and Paris have reduced the time it takes to reach Madeira from three and a half days by ship to virtually the same number of hours by air. Other services, involving a change to a connecting service at Lisbon, link twenty-eight Continental cities with the island. Cruise liners are now the most common vessels to be seen in Funchal Bay—but, if the time is right, passengers still like to come ashore and savour the ritual pleasure of tea, cucumber sandwiches and Madeira cake on the terrace at Reid's.

Afternoon tea at Reid's Hotel is served in the lounge and on the terrace. The menu includes bread and butter with jam, marmalade or honey, sandwiches, cakes, pastries and ice-cream. Tea, coffee, chocolate and fruit juices are available.

SAVIOUR OF THE WORLD

In 1949, his seventy-fifth year, Winston Churchill suffered a minor stroke. By the autumn he had made an excellent recovery, but it was decided that he would benefit from a winter holiday. He therefore sent a cable in November to Bryce Nairn, the British consul at an island he had last visited half a century earlier, in October 1899, on his way to South Africa to cover the Boer War as a correspondent for the newspaper the *Morning Post*—Madeira. His cable said: 'Query warm, paintable, bathable, comfortable, flowery, hotels, etc . . . Keep all secret. Should so much like to see you both again.'

Six years earlier, Bryce Nairn had been the consul at Marrakesh in Morocco when Churchill, returning from the first 'Big Three' conference with Roosevelt and Stalin at Teheran, was stricken by pneumonia at Carthage and, for a time, feared to be on the point of death. He survived the attack, however, and chose to recuperate over the New Year of 1944 in the Moroccan southern capital. His stay in Marrakesh forged an enduring friendship with Bryce Nairn and his wife, Margaret, who shared Churchill's enthusiasm for painting and had been a professional artist before her marriage. In 1945, while awaiting the result of the post-war general election, at which the electorate decided that the right man for the war was the wrong man for the peace and presented the Labour Party with a landslide victory, Churchill had spent a short holiday at Bordeaux, where Bryce Nairn had been posted. Now he had sought their guidance about whether Madeira would be a suitable place to relax, enjoy some sunshine, paint and, in addition, work on the fourth volume of his war memoirs, *The Hinge of Fate*.

Bryce Nairn recommended Reid's, which was both an honour and to some extent an embarrassment. The hotel had only just reopened its doors after being on a care-and-maintenance basis for nine years because of

Mr and Mrs Winston Churchill at Reid's Hotel in January 1950.

the war. Yet great hotels are expected to—and usually do—rise to the occasion. Plans were sent of a suite that could be made available; British residents in Madeira donated elegant pieces of their own favourite furniture to ensure that it was fitting for the greatest living Englishman of the century.

Churchill set sail on 29 December, 1949, in the Union-Castle liner *Durban Castle*, and arrived at Funchal on 2 January, 1950. His extensive party included his wife, his daughter Diana (Mrs Duncan Sandys, the wife of a British Conservative politician), his literary assistant Bill Deakin, two secretaries, two Special Branch detectives and a manservant, who was planning to leave his service at the end of a trip which proved to be considerably shorter than had been intended originally.

It was already dark when the Churchill party came ashore on 2 January, but Madeira was aglow with its traditional and extravagant New Year illuminations which increase the island's consumption of electricity by forty per cent. An enormous electric V-sign shone on the roof of the Blandy offices, where the great majority of the island's British residents and holiday-makers had gathered to greet the man to whom the free world owed so much. News of his visit had also drawn a large crowd of Madeirans, who stood at first in silence, which is the Portuguese way of showing respect, but were swift to join in once the British community began to cheer and clap.

At Reid's, Mr and Mrs Churchill were given a standing ovation when they made their entry into the dining-room, where the manager, John Paquot, previously assistant to the legendary Luigi Gandolfo, made a brief speech of welcome and asked the other guests diplomatically to do all they could to respect the Churchills' desire for a quiet holiday and to take as little notice of them as possible. They occupied rooms on the ground floor, known today as the 'Churchill Suite', which had been the holiday home a quarter of a century earlier of Mr and Mrs David Lloyd George and would later be occupied by another British Prime Minister, the Earl of Avon—better known as Anthony Eden—and his wife.

In addition to working on his war memoirs, Churchill set out to paint at the nearby fishing village of Camara de Lobos, where the spot he set up his easel is today marked by a plaque. For transportation he had the use of a grey Rolls-Royce belonging to the Leacocks, another of Madeira's distinguished families. 'My father lent him the car and his chauffeur, Joaquim, and provided a picnic,' explained William Leacock. 'He also equipped the boot of the Rolls as a bar. Mr Churchill liked a drink when he was painting.'

At Reid's, by and large, the Churchills kept out of the way of other guests. 'They usually ate in their suite,' said Joseph, later the famous hall porter, who was then working in room service. 'My brother was head waiter at the time and asked me to look after the Churchill Suite.' He performed the task so efficiently that Churchill invited him to return to London and enter his employment.

'I asked for twenty-four hours to think the matter over,' Joseph went on. 'I also sought the advice of the manservant he had brought with him. He said: "It's up to you, but I'm leaving as soon as we go back to London because of all the work. Every day there are banquets—banquets at breakfast, banquets at lunch, banquets at afternoon tea, banquets at dinner, banquets at supper. I'm on my feet all day and I can't stand it any more."'

Joseph understood the cause of complaint. 'Looking after the Churchill Suite and its occupants, I was starting work at six o'clock in the morning and often did not leave the hotel until midnight. I was tired. I told Mr Churchill the next day that, because of the physical conditions, I did not wish to take the post he had offered me. He said: "I thought that would be your answer. It's a pity because I should have liked you to come."'

It was not always easy not to take notice of Churchill. At a dinner British residents gave in his honour at Reid's, he was enchanted to learn that one of the Madeira wines being served dated from 1792, a particularly fine vintage, and had a distinguished history of its own. It had formed part of a pipe of wine (105 gallons) delivered to HMS *Northumberland*, the naval vessel taking Napoleon into exile at St Helena in 1815—an unhappy experience for Henry Veitch, the British consul in Madeira, who accompanied the wine on board and was reprimanded because he disobeyed orders from Whitehall and addressed the former French emperor as 'Your Majesty' instead of 'General'.

Napoleon, who suffered from a gastric complaint, was not allowed to drink the wine and, as nobody had paid for it, it was returned after his death in 1820 to the Madeira merchant who had supplied it. Eventually the wine, by then bottled, was sold to Charles Blandy in

The Rolls-Royce lent by the Leacock family to Churchill for the duration of his stay in Madeira. *Photo: Alexes Weaver*

1922. On hearing the intriguing story of the wine's history, Churchill announced: 'Ladies and gentlemen, here is a famous wine indeed, vintaged when Marie Antoinette was still alive'—and, placing a napkin over one arm, served the assembled guests himself.

What had been planned as an extended working holiday had to be cut short after only nine days. The Parliament elected in 1945 was nearing the end of its five-year term and Clement Attlee, the Labour Prime Minister, announced its Dissolution and set 23 February as the date for a general election. Churchill took the flying-boat from Funchal to Southampton to start the campaign that was to result in another Tory defeat, but by the much narrower margin of only six seats. Local dignitaries gathered on the quayside to bid him farewell. 'But before he finally left he made a point of singling out Joaquim and thanking him for being his chauffeur during his short stay,' said William Leacock, 'I think it was a kind gesture from a great man.'

Golden Names from a Golden Century

Golden Names from a Golden Century

Empress Elizabeth of Austria

First Earl Roberts, *British field marshal, C.-in.-C. of the British Army from 1900 to 1905*

Sir (Joseph) Austen Chamberlain, *British statesman whose posts included Chancellor of the Exchequer, Foreign Secretary and First Lord of the Admiralty*

Duke of Connaught and Strathearn, *seventh child and third son of Queen Victoria*, and his wife, the Duchess

Duchess of Aosta

Ex-Emperor Karl and ex-Empress Zita of Austria

Prince Maximilian of Habsburg

Duchess of Parma

David Lloyd George, *British statesman*, and his family: *as Chancellor of the Exchequer, he introduced old age pensions and health and employment insurance, and was made a peer shortly before his death in 1945*

First Earl of Birkenhead (F. E. Smith), *lawyer and British statesman*, his wife, the Countess, and his daughter, Lady Pamela Smith

George Bernard Shaw, *Irish dramatist*

Maharajah Gaekwar of Baroda

Duke of Westminster

Mr and Mrs John Bailey, *the latter one of Winston Churchill's daughters*, on their honeymoon

Princess Marie-Louise, *daughter of Queen Victoria*

Amy Mollison (*née* Johnson), *pioneer flyer*

Prince George, Duke of Kent

Princess Helena, *daughter of Queen Victoria*

Rainer Maria Rilke, *poet*

Prince Negus, *son of Emperor Haile Selasse of Ethiopia*

Winston Churchill

Prince Axel of Denmark

Guglielmo Marconi, *Italian pioneer in the invention and development of wireless telegraphy: when he tried to interest a London newspaper in his invention, a reporter sent downstairs to talk to him returned with the message: 'It's just some lunatic foreigner who thinks he can send a message from one room to another'*

Guests at Reid's Hotel celebrating the marriage of HRH Princess Margaret with Mr Anthony Armstrong-Jones in May 1960. *Photo: Museu Vicentes*

The Duke of Devonshire

Benno Moiseiwitsch, *Russian pianist, known for his rendering of the works of the Romantics*

Doña Carmen Polo de Franco

Pedro de Freitas Branco, *composer*

Ex-King Umberto, *the last king of Italy*

Gregory Peck, *actor*

The Count and Countess of Barcelona

Dr Marcello Caetano, *Portuguese lawyer and statesman, who became Prime Minister in 1968*

First Earl of Halifax, *British statesman who served as Foreign Secretary and was also Britain's ambassador in the United States for the greater part of the Second World War*, and his wife, the Countess

Princess Maria Pia of Savoy

Prince Alexandre of Yugoslavia

Marquis and Marchioness of Villaverde

General Fulgençio Batista, *deposed dictator of Cuba*, and his family

Sacheverell Sitwell, *British art critic, poet and author*

Albert Schweitzer, *French theologian, organist and missionary surgeon*

Duke of Bragança, *a descendant of the family that ruled Portugal from 1640 to 1853*

Marquis of Pombal

John dos Passos, *American author*

Cyril Lord, *British industrialist*, and Mrs Lord

Archduchess Regina of Austria-Hungary

Roger Moore, *British actor*

A. J. Cronin, *Scottish author*

Queen Ingrid of Denmark

Prince George of Denmark

King Carlos Gustav XVI and Queen Silvia of Sweden

Baron Butler of Saffron Walden, *British statesman whose posts included Chancellor of the Exchequer, Foreign Secretary and deputy Prime Minister*, and Baroness Butler

Sir Bernard Docker, *company chairman and director*, and Lady Docker

Archduke Rudolf of Habsburg

Above: HRH the Count of Barcelona with HRH Princess Gabriela of Savoy in August 1966.

Below: The American writer John dos Passos with Mr Jean Burca, manager of Reid's Hotel, and his wife, in July 1960. *Photo: Museu Vicentes*

The Earl and Countess of Avon, who visited Reid's Hotel in 1973.

THE SLIP OF A KNIFE

The slip of a surgeon's knife brought to a premature end the distinguished political career of Sir Anthony Eden, later the Earl of Avon. He had three spells in office as Britain's Foreign Secretary—1935 to 1938, when he resigned over the Government's decision to open talks with the Italian dictator, Mussolini; 1940 to 1945, taking part in all the great conferences of the Second World War; and 1951 to 1955, when he succeeded Winston Churchill as Britain's Prime Minister.

In August 1952 he was married for the second time, to Churchill's niece Clarissa. Twelve months later he underwent a gall bladder operation which was bungled. Despite further operations to try to put the matter right, his health gradually deteriorated and, suffering from recurrent severe fevers, he finally resigned shortly after the Suez crisis of 1956, when President Nasser of Egypt seized the Suez canal.

In retirement, he and his wife took to wintering abroad for the sake of his health. Their holidays included visits to Portugal, where they had also spent their honeymoon, and a stay as guests at Reid's in 1973. The appeal of Portugal, he once wrote to Baron Beaverbrook, the Canadian newspaper millionaire, lay in the fact that he liked the 'food, wine and people, and the general atmosphere of a hundred years ago'.

SAND IN HIS SHOES

As befitted such an auspicious occasion, the senior members of the staff of Reid's were in position to receive their distinguished guest. Local dignatories had assembled. The security men and the police were in their appointed places. But where was the distinguished guest?

The answer? Forty miles away on the neighbouring island of Porto Santo where he had just been delivered by the US Air Force and, on descending from the aircraft, had commented: 'This can't be Madeira—there's too much sand.'

Viscount Carrington, then Secretary-General of NATO, had decided at the end of a European tour to spend a few days relaxing at Reid's. The US Air Force kindly offered to give him a lift. 'Unfortunately,' he says, 'they thought I wanted to visit the NATO base on Porto Santo.'

All was well that ended well—but it was three hours before the distinguished guest arrived to enjoy his few days' rest.

Viscount Carrington, whose holiday at Reid's Hotel began with an unexpected diversion.

Terry Thomas, *Australian actor*

Princess Pilar Bourbon

Princess Gabriela of Savoy

Sir Ralph Richardson, *British actor*, and Lady Richardson

Archduke Otto of Habsburg

Princess Elizabeth of Liechtenstein

Baron George-Brown, *British politician whose posts included Foreign Secretary*

Sir Roy Welensky, *Rhodesian statesman and heavyweight boxing champion who became his country's Prime Minister*

Viscount and Viscountess Boyd of Merton

Lady Spencer Churchill

Peter Walker, MP, *British politician and former Secretary of State for Wales*

Ian Smith, *Prime Minister of Rhodesia, who made a unilateral declaration of independence in 1965*

The Earl (Anthony Eden) and Countess of Avon: *Long-serving statesman Lord Avon had three spells as Britain's Foreign Secretary, including five wartime years, and succeeded Churchill (Lady Avon was his niece) as Prime Minister in 1955, resigning shortly after the Suez Canal crisis of the following year*

Baron Widgery, *former Lord Chief Justice of England*, and Baroness Widgery

The Earl and Countess of Dundee

Gordon Jackson, *Scottish actor*

The Earl and Countess of Munster

The Earl and Countess of Wemyss

Duchess of Somerset

Pik Botha, *Prime Minister and later president of South Africa*

Viscount Carrington, *Secretary General of NATO*

Reid's Hotel

1891 - 1991